THE FORGOTTEN NAME

A GUIDED REFLECTION ON REMEMBRANCE

DERNY-JEAN

Preface

There are truths so ancient, so deep, that they do not need to be taught—only remembered.

This diary is not here to give you answers, nor does it ask you to abandon what you already know. Instead, it invites you into a space of questioning, reflection, and rediscovery—a journey not toward something new, but toward something you may have always known, buried beneath the noise of history, tradition, and war.

The story of *The Forgotten Name* is more than just a tale of a distant kingdom—it is a mirror. It asks us to look at the world we live in, the beliefs we hold, and at the cycles we repeat. It challenges us to ask:

- What if war is not divine, but a choice?
- What if the divisions we accept as natural were once unknown?
- What if the voice of wisdom was never lost—only silenced?

Following the story, you will find 30 days of reflective questions—not to test you, but to guide you. Some may be easy to answer, others may challenge everything you have believed. But each one is a step toward uncovering your own truth.

Take your time.

Be honest with yourself. And as you move through these pages, listen not just to the words, but to the silence in between.

For it is there, in that silence, that the Name waits to be spoken again.

May you remember.

The Forgotten Name

Long ago, in a land of vast mountains and flowing rivers, there was a kingdom that had stood for generations. Its people were proud, its warriors strong, and its rulers wise—at least, that is what they believed.

At the heart of the kingdom stood a grand temple, a place of worship dedicated to the ***One True God***. The priests taught that their people were chosen, blessed above all others, and that their God had given them strength to rule the land.

But the kingdom was always at war.

The enemies of the kingdom, they claimed, were wicked. They worshiped false gods, defied the natural order, and sought to take what was not theirs. For as long as anyone could remember, the kingdom fought to protect its land, its honor, and its sacred destiny.

And so, war became a way of life. Fathers trained their sons for battle. Mothers hardened their hearts, knowing their children would either fight or perish. The blacksmiths forged weapons before farming tools, and the scribes recorded victories before history.

One day, an old traveler arrived in the city. He carried no weapon, only a simple walking stick. His beard was long, his robe was worn, and his eyes held the weight of many lifetimes.

He entered the grand temple, where the king and his priests were gathered, praying for victory in the next great battle.

"Who do you pray to?" the traveler asked.

The high priest glared at him. "We pray to the One True God—the God of our people, the God of strength and justice!"

The traveler nodded. "And what do you ask of this God?"

"That He grant us victory over our enemies," the king declared. "That He guide us to glory and crush those who stand against us!"

The traveler sighed. "And if your enemies pray to the same God? If they too ask for victory?"

The priests scoffed. "Our God is with us, not them!"

The traveler smiled sadly. Then, in a voice as soft as a whisper yet heavy as a storm, he spoke a Name.

It was not a name the people had heard before, yet it was familiar. It carried warmth, like the first light of dawn, and weight, like the roots of an ancient tree. The walls of the temple seemed to breathe at the sound of it.

The laughter died in the priests' throats. The soldiers standing guard tensed, their hands gripping their weapons. A hush fell over the temple, thick as mist before the rain.

The high priest took a step forward, his voice trembling. "That name... it is forbidden."

.

"Why?" the traveler asked.

The priest lowered his gaze. "Because it is the Name before the war. The Name before we were chosen, before we were divided. It is the Name of the God who belongs to all."

A murmur spread through the gathered crowd. Some looked confused. Others looked afraid.

The traveler nodded. "And why did you forbid it?"

The priest swallowed hard. "Because it made war impossible."

A long silence followed.

The gathered priests, warriors, and nobles stood still, as if the air itself had thickened. Some looked at one another, waiting for someone to speak. But no one did.

Outside, the great bells of the temple chimed, marking the hour. Their echoes stretched through the city, reaching the ears of soldiers sharpening their swords, merchants preparing supplies for the war campaign, and children playing in the dust, too young to understand the cost of the battles waged in their names.

Within the temple, the traveler's words hung in the air, as heavy as the stone pillars that had stood for centuries.

The oldest among the priests furrowed his brow. He had lived through many wars, watched the kingdom rise and fall, and blessed countless soldiers as they marched to -

battle. And yet, as he stood there, he found that he could not remember the first enemy, the first battle, the first drop of blood that had ever been spilled in the name of war.

Had there ever been a beginning? Or had they been fighting for so long that war itself had become the only truth they knew?

A soldier shifted uneasily, his fingers tightening around the hilt of his sword. He had killed men whose faces he barely remembered. He had watched his friends die in his arms. He had always believed it was righteous, that it was for the will of God.

But now... now he wondered.

"If the Name before war had once been known, and if it had to be forbidden so that it would be forgotten—so that war could continue—then what did that mean?"

A cold ripple passed through the temple.

The king, feeling the weight of the silence pressing against him, squared his shoulders. He could see the doubt creeping into the eyes of his people. He could hear the hesitation in the breath of the priests who had always spoken with certainty.

Something deep inside him—something he had long buried—whispered that the traveler was right.

But he could not allow it.

If they were not chosen, if war was not their purpose, if their victories were not the will of God... then what had they been fighting for?

His hands curled into fists, his voice breaking the silence like the crack of a whip.

"If we are not chosen, then what are we?"

The traveler looked at him, his gaze steady. "You are stewards, not conquerors. You are brothers to your enemies, not their masters. You are children of the same creation, not rulers of it."

The murmurs grew louder. Some of the warriors stepped back. A few priests exchanged uneasy glances.

The king's face darkened. "Then why have we fought for generations? Why have we shed blood in His name?"

The traveler's voice was calm, unshaken.

"Because it was never His will, but yours."

The king's face twisted with anger, but there was doubt in his eyes.

The traveler turned to leave. "You may continue your war, if you wish. But if you ever wish to know peace, speak the Name again—not in prayer for victory, but in remembrance of who you were before war defined you."

And with that, he stepped out of the temple, disappearing into

And with that, he stepped out of the temple, disappearing into the city streets.

Epilogues: The Name in the Wind

For many nights after the traveler left, the temple remained quiet.

The priests still led prayers, but their voices trembled where once they had thundered. The soldiers still sharpened their swords, but their hands hesitated. The people still spoke of war, but now, for the first time, they also spoke of the Name.

Some refused to say it, afraid of what it might undo. Others whispered it in secret, as though testing the weight of a long-forgotten truth. A few spoke it boldly, and to their surprise, the sky did not darken, nor did the earth tremble in wrath.

The king, in the solitude of his chambers, sat before a map covered in the marks of battles past and battles planned. He had spent his life ruling by the sword, believing that the strength of his kingdom was in its victories.

But now, for the first time, he asked himself: *What would my kingdom be without war?*

No one had ever imagined it.

And in the deep silence of the night, when even the torches burned low, the wind carried something unseen through the city streets. It slipped through doorways and into the ears of those half-dreaming.

It wove through the marketplace, through the fields, through the homes of those who had lost sons and fathers to war.

It carried no command, no decree—only a Name.

A Name that had been buried beneath the weight of centuries.

A Name that, once spoken, could not be forgotten again.

And though the kingdom did not change overnight, though wars were not instantly halted, and though many clung tightly to the old ways, something had shifted.

For the first time, war was not a certainty.

For the first time, the people wondered if there was another way.

And for the first time, the Name was spoken not in defiance, nor in secrecy—

but in hope.

GUIDED REFLECTION: THE NAME BEFORE WAR

The story of *The Forgotten Name* is not just about a kingdom—
it is about all of us. It asks us to reconsider the beliefs we
inherit, the cycles we repeat, and the choices we make. In the
following pages are 30 thought-provoking questions designed
to help you explore your own insights.

Take your time with each question. Write down your answers,
discuss them with others, or simply reflect in silence. There
are no right or wrong responses—only paths to deeper
understanding.

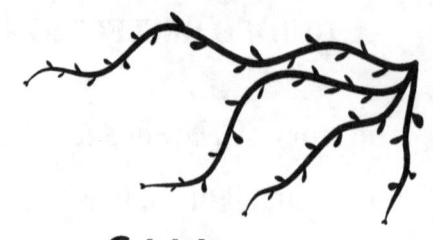

The Weight of War

What do you think kept the kingdom in a constant state of war? Was it truly their enemies, or something else?

Do you think war is inevitable or is it a choice? What does history suggest?

Who benefit the most from war? Who suffers the most?

How has war (or the idea of it) shaped your understanding of power?

If war suddenly became impossible, what would leaders
and nations do instead?

The kingdom in the story believed their enemies were "wicked." How often are conflicts fueled by the belief that the other side is evil rather than simply different?

Think of conflicts in history. How many were fought for survival, and how many were fought for control?

What are some ways societies could resolve conflict without war?

If peace were prioritized as much as war, what kind of advancements might humanity achieve?

The Forgotten Name

What do you think the "Name" in the story represents?
Does it have meaning beyond just a forgotten word?

Why do you think the priests feared the Name? What would it have changed?

Have you ever questioned something you were taught to believe as absolute truth? What happened when you did?

How do religious or cultural identities sometimes contribute to division instead of unity?

Is it possible for a belief system to unite people without creating an "us vs them" mentality? What would that look like?

What does it mean to be "chosen"? Is it a divine truth or a human idea?

If God truly favored one people over another, what would
that say about the nature of God?

Many faiths claim their followers are special or chosen. What happens when different groups claim this at the same time?

How might a God who belongs to all of humanity be
different from a God of only one group?

If you could hear the voice of the divine, what do you think it would say about war?

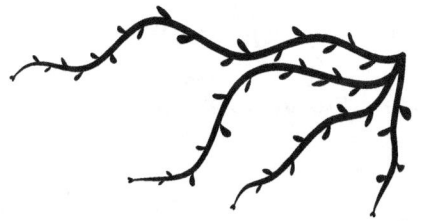

BREAKING THE CYCLE + REIMAGINING THE FUTURE

The king asked, "If we are not chosen, then what are we?" How would you answer him?

If a leader decided to reject war and pursue peace, what resistance might they face? From whom?

The traveler says, "You are stewards, not conquerors."
What does it mean to be a steward rather than an
owner?

What would a world without war actually look like? How would power work?

What steps can individuals take to break cycles of division, even in their own communities?

The wind carried the Name through the city, slowly shifting minds. What do you think this represents?

What does it take for people to let go of old beliefs and embrace new ones?

Is true peace possible in our lifetime? Why or why not?

If you had to create a "monument to peace" instead of war, what would it look like?

How will this story change the way you think about war,
faith and humanity's future?

The Forgotten Name

Final Reflection:

The journey toward truth is not about finding easy answers—it is about asking deeper questions. Which of these questions challenged you the most? Which ones gave you new insights? Remember, change does not happen overnight, but it begins with a shift in thought. Like the people in the story, we each have a choice: to continue the cycles of war, division, and fear—or to whisper the Forgotten Name and begin to remember. What will you choose?